Look Up High

Written by Hawys Morgan

Collins

At night, it is dark.

Look up. You can see the moon.

The Big Dipper shimmers.

You can see it on the chart, too.

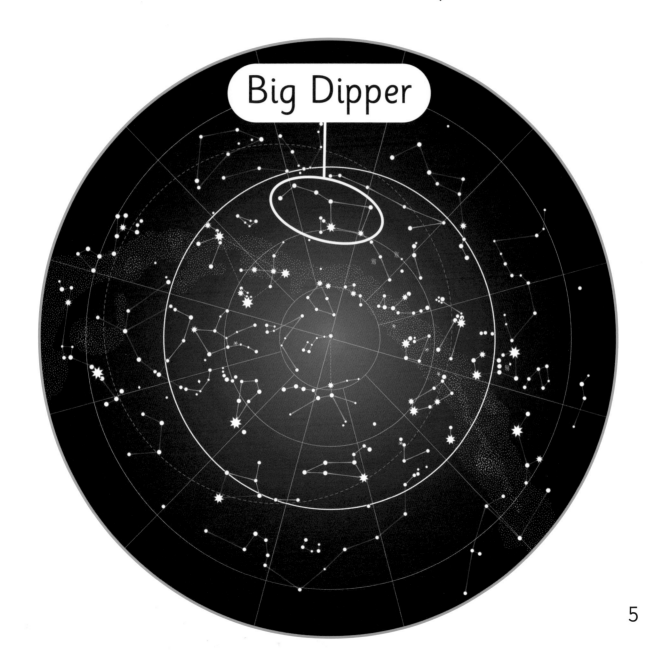

Big Dipper

Look at Mars!

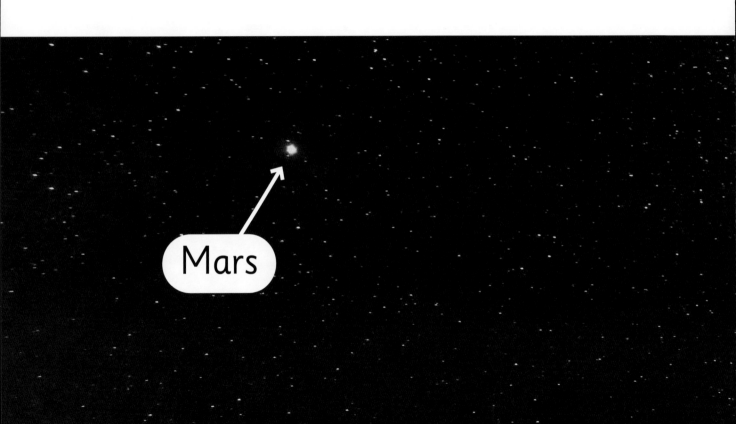

The rocks and soil are red on Mars.

Look at Saturn.

It has rings.

Look up high. Wow!

A burning rock shoots by. It is a comet!

The northern lights shimmer in the dark.

You see terrific lights at night!

Look up high

🐾 Review: After reading 🐾

Use your assessment from hearing the children read to choose any GPCs, words or tricky words that need additional practice.

Read 1: Decoding

- Discuss the meaning of **rings** on page 9. Ask: Where are the rings? (e.g. *around Saturn*)
- Talk about what these rings might be made from (*rocks*) compared with other rings they are aware of. (e.g. *gold jewellery*)
- Ask the children to sound out these words that have more than one syllable. Can they identify the digraphs that make the /er/ and /ur/ sounds?

Dipper	**Saturn**	**burning**
shimmers	**northern**	

- Challenge the children to pick a label and read it fluently. Ask: Can you blend the sounds in your head when you read the label?

Read 2: Prosody

- Challenge the children to use an expressive voice, like a television presenter, to read pages 6 and 7.
- Encourage the children to use a commanding tone for page 6, to grab the listener's attention.
- Before reading page 7, discuss which word might be the most surprising to listeners and so worth extra emphasis. (*red*)

Read 3: Comprehension

- Ask the children if they have seen any of the things discussed in this book in the sky at night. Can they name and describe what they saw? How did they feel when they saw it?
- Talk about what other titles the book could have, for example, *The Night Sky*; *Outer Space*.
- Look at pages 4 to 7, and for each double page ask questions focusing on the main idea, and what else we learn. For example, on pages 4 and 5:
  - What is the main subject here? (*a pattern of stars called the Big Dipper*)
  - What extra information do we learn about the Big Dipper? (*it shimmers; it's on a chart*)
- Turn to pages 14–15 and ask the children to tell you about any pictures of their choice.